25 Things to Keep in Mind
During a Pandemic
…or any Ole Time

Marty Herzog

In loving gratitude for all my teachers.

There have been many times in my life when I've wished for some kind of giant pause button to be pushed so everything that was happening would just stop for a while. Expectations at work would become more and more difficult. Time never slowed down with Friday turning into another Monday and weekends being a blur of a multitude of tasks needing to be taken care of with only a few precious hours to try to make some fun. So when that pause finally did happen under the guise of an unexpected global pandemic, I actually wasn't prepared for it.

Because this was not pondering my life over a favorite dish at a restaurant or while taking a stroll down the beach. This was go home and stay home and confront my mortality and every single life choice I ever made. For months. And months. And oh look, summer has gone by.

'You don't know what you have until it's gone' sounds like a nice platitude until what you have is actually gone. Especially when it's something you never in a million years thought would be gone. You want to be mad at yourself that you never took the time to consider those things not being around for you. But how could you? How could you predict the only life you've ever known would be something that's no longer available to you the way it used to be?

The mind doesn't know how to process an unprecedented event such as a global pandemic so it's going to need to work in ways it hasn't before. Give it some space and let it do what it needs to do. This is a level of trauma and loss and anxiety that you have not dealt with before. Expecting your mind to cope with this in the ways it always has is not a reasonable expectation. Likewise, your behavior is going to change some also. You may sleep more and have vivid dreams, you may remember past events you have not thought of in many years, or you may become surprisingly emotional. Give yourself the understanding and room to cope with this added upheaval and give the people around you the same courtesy.

This pandemic is unique, but any life crisis can have a similar effect. Here is a list of 25 things you can keep in mind during those times or really in any circumstance.

Each section is going to be a reflection of my construct of the world. But like Horatio said to Hamlet, there are more things in heaven and earth that are dreamt of in my philosophy. Every person has their own take on how this life works primarily based on their own experiences. You don't have to buy into everything that is said here to get something out of it. Pick and choose as you may. What is important, though, is that you begin to realize how it is you understand the world, for all your behaviors are going to stem from that including your unconscious habits and most importantly your thoughts.

All my life I've been a seeker and have found these topics to be truth for me. They are presented here in this straightforward, no frills book with the hope that you will get something out of them too.

1

Accept, release, surrender.

I do not like these three words when facing a difficult and hurtful situation. When you're in a great deal of pain, what you want is one thing and one thing only: for the pain to end. You do not want to have to embrace these three words.

There's a lot of stomping, crying and blaming you can do. But when that's all out of you and the situation has not gone away and is still staring you down, it does slowly start to sink in that this really is the only option you have.

But, and here's the rub, you have to truly embrace these three words. I like to tell myself that sure I accept this situation. But really I haven't. Because it needs to be accepted on its terms, not on mine. It is making the rules. It is its way or the highway and I am finally agreeing that yes, that's the path I'm going to take.

This is a great blow to the ego whose terms must always be the ones that are obeyed. Once the situation's terms are accepted, the ego is not in control anymore. It does not like that. But the dance has begun, you say you're in acceptance, but you aren't completely. Then you accept some more although there's still a bit you don't, and this continues until you finally do embrace it.

Accept. If you do not fully accept the present moment that you're experiencing, there's nothing else to move on to. As you begin this process, the pain of the situation will remind you that it's still there. But the more and more you focus on accepting, the hurt begins to change and feel different. It is in that acceptance that you are allowing for possibilities to enter that could not get in before. There is now extra room for resolutions you didn't know existed.

Release. Just let it go. It certainly does not feel good, so simply let go like you do a balloon in the breeze. When you start to let go of your grip, it starts to let go of its grip.
Even though it might still feel that it's right there, you're no longer grasping onto it. While doing this, make it a practice to focus on your breath. Slowly inhale and exhale. Let yourself relax as you feel the tightening diminish.

Surrender. You're not giving up. You're letting it be what it needs to be without trying to define it. You are choosing to be free, and in that freedom you can find new ways of being and operating you didn't know were available to you.

2
Be grateful.

Only always.

Science teaches that everything in our universe is made up of submicroscopic particles. In physical objects that appear to be solid, the particles are tightly packed together but are actually vibrating in place. In lighter states such as gasses, the particles are moving around and vibrating more quickly. Our thoughts are no different, they too vibrate at different frequencies. Low-level thoughts such as anger and jealousy are vibrating at a lower frequency, and high-level thoughts such as gratitude and thankfulness vibrate at a higher frequency.

Just like the radio where you can tune into any type of station you want, you can have any kind of experience you want by the level of vibration you choose to emit and thus attract. One rule of the universe is that like attracts like. A vibration of hatred is going to attract things similar to that vibration which can be described as bad. A vibration of love is going to attract things similar to that vibration which can be described as good. For whatever reason, gratitude is that turbo charged vibration that summons more and more of what it is you are being grateful for.

Let being grateful be the last thing on your mind as you fall asleep and the first thing you think of when you wake up. Be so excited when there's a line you have to wait in because it's going to give you extra time to go over the list of all the things you're grateful for.

It is not that we are in a constant state of hope that we will at some point experience abundance, but rather that we have an on-going attitude of gratitude now. Then events happen that bring about more and more of that abundance which is everyone's birthright. Being grateful is a conscious decision especially when all kinds of roadblocks appear. When the going gets tough, the tough get grateful.

It is the best way to engage our minds so that the best things can manifest for us.

3
Forgive.

Forgiveness is the most misunderstood of actions. It is highly transformative. If done correctly and consistently, it will change your life for the better exponentially.

People think forgiveness is everything that it is not. That it is contingent upon an apology before it is granted. That it gets to come with a heaping helping of judgement for who needs to be forgiven. That there's a secret compartment inside where we get to hide some distain for the offender.

The ego simply won't allow for real forgiveness and will disguise it in the aforementioned ways and a host of others.

True forgiveness is acting as if the offense never happened. If it never happened, there's no need for any of the drama surrounding it. If it never occurred, the other person is free and clear. Period.

Although it doesn't mean that you put yourself back in the same situation where it could happen again. Stay clear of scenarios in which you can be hurt. Live and learn, mate.

Be in a constant state of forgiveness regarding all things both in the present moment and in the past. Remember, for forgiveness to truly work the miracles that it can and will, it is as if the offending occurrence is not real.

We forgive so we can move on and truly be free. It has nothing to do with the person who committed the seeming offense. Hanging onto grudges and resentment is going to keep us locked in levels of hell where we will stay for a very long time. It will prevent us from living the beautiful life we were intended to live.

The best and only revenge is to forgive. If you're one of those people whose purpose in life is to make others learn their lesson, the best way to do that is to learn yours and forgive.

4
Have no attachment to an outcome.

This is a foreign concept to many of us. It is always helpful to decipher what our motivations truly are. I realize that I am certainly willing to go the extra mile—but if I get recognition for it. I am willing to help you out when you need it—if you never forget it. I'll make the decision to always do the right thing even when no one is watching—if something really good happens to me down the line.

No matter what it is that you are trying to achieve, be it big or small, do not be invested in a specific outcome. Do all the things that you need to do in order to get what you desire without expecting the result you so desperately want. You actually block the receiving of your desires when you hold on so tightly to your expectations. Get yourself in the correct mindset and joyfully do whatever actions are required and then let the outcome be whatever it's going to be.

That same idea applies if you are trying to change something about yourself. You will never affect that change unless you first unconditionally accept yourself exactly the way you are.

If you are using visualization or a vision board to achieve a means…same thing. Those are great activities, just be detached while doing them. Visualize what brings you freedom with no attachment to a specific outcome.

In all things have no expectations.

It feels like we're going to have to don monk's robes and move to a deserted island to fully embrace this, but we can learn to do it. It is a practice. We may never do it 100% consistently, but over time we will get closer to emptying our mind and just letting the result be what it's going to be.

5
Don't push or force.

It's quite normal when starting something new that we're excited about to become gung-ho and jump right in. Self-improvement is certainly something to be enthused about, but it comes with a catch. It's best we take it nice and easy. Trying to pound these or any points into our heads is going to have a counterproductive effect.

Slow and steady does indeed win the race. Taking on too much too quickly can have the opposite effect of what you're trying to accomplish.

It's helpful to visualize life being like a metronome or a pendulum on a grandfather clock. All the great positive work we are doing on ourselves has an upswing that is going to absolutely help. But there's always a downswing, a counterbalance until it evens out. Allow for some time and turbulence as our old destructive ways are being transformed to new and productive ones that will benefit us. Let it take the time that it needs to get sorted out.

There is a Zen saying that if you find yourself in a place of forcing, empty your rice bowl. Take on the mindset of a beginner. Making it a practice to empty your mind makes room for great clarity and many other blessings including good health.

Constantly work on being the best version of yourself you can be, but be gentle about it. You're unlearning old habits; you're breaking through the cobwebs in your minds where old tapes have played for years and years and have taken hold. Like a surgeon, explore and cut out what needs to be removed, but use precision and take your time. The ironic thing is that having this mindset will actually save you time in the long run.

6
Feel good.

Only always.

The best environment to affect lasting change is in a mind that is consistently feeling good. Constantly being angry, hateful or worried is going to have unintended negative consequences and block the beautiful life experiences we all deserve to have.

Each positive thought we have and action we do contributes to our abundance and well-being. Uplifting constructive thoughts and actions attract like experiences. We've all had days where first thing something goes wrong and the whole day goes downhill from there. The converse is true also when we immediately start our day by intentionally feeling good. Constantly focus on the task at hand and feel good about it.

What is a beneficial thing to listen to first thing in the morning that lifts your spirits—inspirational music, a favorite author, an inspiring podcast? What mood enhancing exercise is best—a walk, yoga, biking? What is a helpful 10-minute meditation—journaling, chanting, emptying your mind of thoughts? When you wake up, there's so much stuff you're bringing back into consciousness with you. Spend some time recognizing what that is and letting it go. Find a healthy way to vent (not to your significant other or dog) and release the negative thoughts. Then keep a good feeling going the entire day.

What is the primary goal for your day? To have a great one! So let go of everything that prevents that from happening. Release reacting in ways that make you feel bad especially in unexpected situations that arise. Recognize the traps you consistently fall into where you react to a situation by feeling awful, and then stop doing that. And if you do still fall into that trap, don't judge yourself. Get back on that horse and start to feel good again.

In addition to being grateful in order to manifest all the good things you want to experience, act "as if". Ask yourself, if you had exactly what you wanted, how would that make you feel? Then feel "as if" you already have those things.

You are of course going to find yourself feeling lousy or in pain at times. It's a matter of allowing yourself to feel that way, then getting yourself back on track as soon as possible to feeling good.

7
Don't be afraid.

Fear is the root of all evil. Fear robs us of the life we could have. Fear lies to us and tells us horror stories of what could happen if we dare try something we have always wanted to do.

Fear gives us a counterfeit life. We think we're living, but actually we're just being afraid and we're exhausted because that takes up so much energy.

Sometimes fear comes into our lives early when we're a child. Sometimes it seeps in later when we're a teenager or young adult facing a new, difficult circumstance. However it finds its way in, it is insidious. It has no other intention than to keep us from being the highest version of ourselves that we can be. It will steal our dreams and take our best relationships. It will keep us from knowing all the resources both internal and external that we have available to us.

Your natural state is one of freedom. Do not let fear take that away from you.

The only time to give it any attention is if your physical safety is being threatened, if you're getting a gut reaction that it is imperative to not go or to leave a situation, or if your life is being threatened. These are healthy responses and you should take action.

But the day-to-day grip that fear wants to hold over you that prevents you from living your best life needs to be let go of.

Ask yourself why is this particular fear you're feeling so painful? What is it I'm really afraid of? Go see a good therapist if needed to get to the root cause of where it is coming from. Read a book on the subject, join a support group, meditate on letting that fear go. Write in your journal about it. Push yourself to do the things you really want to do, yet when it comes time to actually do them, you suddenly become overwhelmed with fear.

Weigh the risks. What's the worst thing that could happen if you put yourself out there and do that thing that you're afraid of doing? Take your life back. You are worth it and so is the life awaiting you beyond that fear.

8
If something defeats you, admit it.

This is only temporarily, please don't give up.

Admit you got defeated in that round. Because if you don't, there's a good chance you're not going to learn from it which is what allows you to come back better. Most everyone wants to immediately get up, dust themselves off and get back at it. But there is very helpful information to be found while you're still on the ground and smarting. Ask yourself what happened and why. Quickly moving on isn't always the best course.

Learn from what stopped you. Then you won't be impeded in that same way again. If it's a mental block within yourself, you need to really explore that so you can let it go.

Be humble. Give props to whatever it is that stopped you in your tracks. Humility is what allows us to truly learn the lessons being taught to us and become wiser.

Do this every time whenever even the smallest setback occurs. Immediately nip in the bud what stopped you so that it doesn't turn into something bigger that will take much longer to come back from.

Once you've done that…go get 'em.

9
At some point you will be betrayed.

You will eventually be betrayed by people in your life in both big and small ways. You won't understand why they did what they did to you and it will hurt. It will seem like there was no rhyme or reason for the assault and you'll reel from it.

Even with no justification for their actions, you have one job to do and that's to get over it and forgive them completely. Let them do what they need to do and bless them.

Just make sure you don't put yourself back into a situation where you are being taken advantage of.

You will feel that you are completely innocent in this provocation. On the level of form, you might be. But in true reality it is helpful to recognize that you are receiving a dose of karmic debt even if it's not coming from the person or situation you expected it to.

We have all done things in our past that we regret and that we wish we hadn't done. It's so easy to forget that and it feels much better to our egos to be the blameless victim.

You may or may not believe in past lives, the idea that we are stuck in a cycle of birth and death until we become enlightened. If you do, it becomes more and more apparent that we have past life karma that we still need to work off in addition to karma from this lifetime, and that the best way to do that is by forgiving the provocateur. If you don't buy into the whole past life thing, know that it's best to realize that being betrayed will happen to you at some point or another and rather than carrying it around with you for a decade or two, accepting and releasing it is the quickest way to move on and be at peace.

10
Accept all beings the way they are.

We all have specific ways we want others to behave, a strict code of ethics that everyone should follow (at times we exempt ourselves from that behavior). When they don't adhere to it, we become irritated and get bent out of shape. We begin to understand how flimsy is the idea that we can control other people much less anything in our lives.

People are not going to act in the ways we want them to. To deal with that grave disappointment, it's really easy to categorize them into any racial bias we may be harboring known or unknown. People are not going to look like us, talk and sound like us, or go about their business in the way we think they should. In our neighborhoods no less! If only people wouldn't act that certain way, we wouldn't get so irritated.

Check yourself. You're you and that's fine. And there are other people who are louder than you and express themselves differently than you and don't appreciate things the way they should like you— and that's just fine too.

They're going to cut you off in traffic. They're going to be annoyingly young or past their prime old. Instead of getting that tightness in your chest, just let them be who they are. Better yet, when they do something you find offensive, instead of giving them guff, give them a blessing. Tell yourself you don't understand what it is to be in their religion or to feel like they do in their culture or to be in the circumstance they find themselves in.

Whether someone wronged you, or even were kind to you, you can say and do this, "I send you health, wealth, happiness, success, love, safety and enlightenment".

In your acceptance of them, you will find a sense of lightness and lasting peace.

11
Admit and apologize for your errors.

We don't want to face our offenses, for they offer a glimpse into what's really going on inside the character we are playing on this planet. Demanding others own up to their misdeeds but unconsciously excusing our own is a great trick of the ego.

While it's best to make an immediate apology to the person you wronged, if you are unable to do that at least admit your shortcomings to yourself. You may not be able to look someone else in the eyes while you say you're sorry, but you can at least look at yourself in the mirror.

There's a rich tradition in America that the manly way to be is to always forge ahead and show no weakness. That's the type of toxic masculinity that is the reason the Me Too movement has come to the forefront and there's a sexual predator serving as the President of the United States as of this writing August 2020.

We are defining who we are by admitting our errors against each other, both in the past and in the present. We are saying we stand on the side of righteousness by humbly asking forgiveness for the pain we have caused others. Not making an honest appraisal of how we wrong other people is a dereliction of our duty.

Make it a part of your mental health routine. What triggers you? What behaviors in others cause you to flip out and sometimes create a scene? Know what makes you want to commit a transgression so you can be on guard not to. Just don't go there.

If you have to be, always be on the receiving end of negative energy, not on the giving end. Don't be an instigator of an altercation. It may feel humiliating in the moment, but it will feel so much better later when you do not return in kind, when you do all you can to deflect an escalating situation.

In addition to asking forgiveness for our mistakes, we need to make sure we are standing up for what is just and fair. There are a number of movements that have risen up and are still relevant today. The movement against the rise of fascism, the civil rights movement, the women's rights moment, the LGBTQ rights movement, the environmental movement, the Black Lives Matter movement. We don't have a choice whether or not we are going to take a stand. By our silence or by our activism, we are shouting out loud as to what side of history we are on.

12
Admit to yourself the character you are playing.

"All the world's a stage and all the men and women merely players" is Shakespeare's apt description of life on this planet.

"Who are you?" asks Lewis Carrolls' caterpillar to Alice and to us. Like an actor would in preparing for a role, what would you list are the attributes of your character? First consider all the thoughts that you think about other people. Do you judge them? Then consider your actions. Are your actions loving or less than loving? Upon closer inspection, is the character you are playing a bad guy masquerading as a good guy? Are you fooling most of the people most of the time including yourself about who you are? Do you have some bad qualities but are they outweighed by the good? Exactly how bad are they? Exactly how good are they?

What motivates you? What is your intention? What do you want? Is there room for improvement? Is there room for an overhaul? (Just don't ask what your job is, what your title is, what kind of car your drive, how many degrees you have.) Make sure you are also recognizing what is so lovable about you and all the good you have brought to people's lives.

From when we are first born, we start to accumulate layers of hurts. Those layers then beget layers of coping mechanisms. Those layers then beget unhealthy ways of acting out. All these layers need to be sanded down. It is a slow and painful process, but it must be done.

Be conscious of the character you are playing and how it operates including your defense mechanisms. Remember that is not the real you, your higher self is. If you don't like what you see now, start turning the dials and become more in line with who you believe you really are. Who you want to be operating as.

Act out of gratitude and love for all beings and for yourself. Start stripping away all that is not really you. Be the light of the world.

13
Accept your lot in life.

You must first accept the thing that you wish to change.

It will do you no good to bemoan the fact that you are not in the place where you want to be. You have to start wherever it is you are.

You might be the top executive in the firm you work at, but when you first walk into a martial arts class, you're a white belt. You may work as a dishwasher, but when you walk through your front door at home, you are the most important thing in the world to every member of your family. You might be an influencer on social media, but when you walk into the grocery store, you're going to have to stand in line to check out like everyone else and wait your turn behind the dishwasher.

This doesn't mean you can't get to a different station in life or that there's anything wrong with wanting a better situation for yourself. It does mean to always keep an accepting and positive attitude in every situation you find yourself in and with every person you find yourself with. You miss many important opportunities when you are constantly trying to get from here to a better there. Stop resenting the position you're currently occupying in whatever group you are a part of in life. Don't judge where it is you are.

The ongoing process of creation has put you exactly where you are today. The next place you go to depends on your willingness to accept and be grateful for where you are right now in the present moment.

You might always be the assistant. You might always be the bridesmaid. You might always be the one moving aside to let another pass by. Whatever it is, just be it. Be happy to do what you do in whatever capacity that is. Even in purely social groups, sometimes a hierarchical structure exists based on some sort of status unique to that group. It seems be the way the ego has arranged life on this earth.

Accept your rank. Salute your superior officers. Offer a steady hand to all. What is worthy of respect is being grounded and reverent regardless of what level you are on.

14
Recognize the sacred in everything.

We have all heard some variation of the phrase 'we are all one'. Most people view that as a metaphor. We're not actually the same thing, but we're all human beings so close enough.

But is there such a thing as a universal consciousness? Are we all one mind but individuating ourselves into a specific nervous system?

You can look at life as everything is separate and doing their own thing. Or you can look at life as everything is connected and actually working together. Viewing it that way, what hurts you hurts me. It makes all the more vital Fannie Lou Hamer's quote, "nobody's free until everybody's free".

Einstein is quoted as saying, "There are two ways to live your life. One is as though nothing is a miracle. The other is as though everything is a miracle." To riff off that, if everything is a miracle, and miracles are sacred, then everything is sacred.

What if we're not just made by God, or Source, what if Source extended of Herself and that's what we really are. The extension of Source. Imbued with the same exact creative power, we're just not the originator. What if everything in this universe, or universes, is actually the extension Source? Rocks, trash, weeds, dust, us. Wouldn't that mean everything is sacred?

It would necessitate that we need to treat everything with respect. We would treat other people, animals, and the ocean in the absolute best way possible. The sacredness in me recognizes the sacredness in you. What a great way to run our affairs, what a great way to write laws, with respect for the dignity of all.

15
Repeat positive affirmations.

Just don't let that be all you do.

Affirmations are a positive declarative statement. "I am rich beyond my wildest dreams." Avoid using the words "no" or "not" which completely confuses the process. Keep it simple, be brief and to the point.

Affirmations are not a panacea. They will only be effective as part of an integrated spiritual program. But done properly, they can be an essential part of transformation that will make your life much better.

As with any mental health practice, the environment in your mind must consistently be a loving one. If you're allowing your mind to be filled with hateful thoughts and anger, what you are trying to accomplish will be sabotaged. Having a bad attitude will derail a spiritual program and the life you want quicker than anything.

Keep at it. Practice makes perfect. There are plenty of affirmations out there, tailor make them to your own unique situation. Be generous in your usage of them always allowing your mind to gently return to them throughout your day.

16
Recognize how you truly feel about yourself.

Your self-image is buried under the accumulation of other people's responses and actions towards you. This lifetime worth of layers, like in sedimentary rocks, is going to take some effort to break through.

Very lovingly allow yourself to just be with the thought of how you really feel about yourself. Take as much time and do as many times as needed. This just involves you exploring your own inner thoughts.

The first messages we receive about ourselves usually comes from our parents. It all starts with mommy and daddy. How could it not, our still maturing minds were vulnerable. Even the best of parents are going to leave a few scars, and all bets are off after that.

What do you think of you? Not what your parent's think, not your teachers, nor your colleagues, nor society. When you visualize yourself going through all the activities of life—what do you think of that person you see?

Do you have compassion? Do you recognize all the places in which you give? Do you recognize all the places in which you take? Do you see what your defense mechanisms are? Do you think you react to stress in a healthy way? Do you want to behave in one way but mostly behave in another?

You're not answering to anyone else, just yourself. Do you feel positive enough about yourself? Are those positive thoughts warranted? Do you see yourself in a negative light? Is that negative light legit though?

You cannot eliminate any bad attributes about yourself if you don't know about them. You cannot build on good attributes about yourself if you can't see any. This is about you getting to know yourself better with a genuine concern and desire to be the highest version of yourself that you can be. True acceptance of yourself can only come about with the acknowledgement of the areas in which you can do better. This is where self-love and self-acceptance begins to grow.

17
Give.

If we are all connected and made of the same stuff as Source, what we do to others we do unto ourselves. Both the bad and the good. One of the most powerful ways we can gain independence is to give without ceasing. Do not give with the expectation to receive back. Give simply because it is joyous to heap abundance onto someone else. To fill a void.

Give of both your money and your time, for both are precious commodities. In doing so, you are defining yourself as generous. You will receive generously in like manner.

If you find there is someone who keeps taking advantage of your charitableness, keep an eye on them. The last thing you want to do is become an enabler to someone's self-destructive behavior. If your intuition is telling you that something doesn't feel right, then put your tithing someplace else.

One of the most holy things to witness is someone who has very little share what they do have. Experiencing that will change you. Remember, it can be very sudden going from having very little to having quite a lot, and vice versa. It can happen in the blink of an eye.

Be mindful of making giving a part of your spiritual program. Rejoice that you have something to share. We continually take turns being in the position of someone who can give and someone who needs to receive. Let us play both sides with grace and humility.

The homeless person you give a dollar to has something to teach you. The child you ceaselessly share your time with has something to teach you. The social program you always support has something to teach you.

18
Admit how other people really see you.

Before the pandemic you were wearing a mask as you interacted with society, just not a physical one. There were, however, tell-tell signs there was some slippage and that people were getting glimpses of the real you. The you that perhaps you didn't want seen.

When we're under a great deal of stress or if we're inebriated, we can say and do things we're later embarrassed by and so we pass it off by saying that really wasn't us. It was the pain or the substance talking. It is helpful to consider that it actually is the real us. Is there an alien living inside that only comes out when we're compromised or under extreme pressure?

Human beings are complicated creatures. We're split and fractured. On our journey of healing, it is our responsibility to put all these pieces back together. Doing that is going to take some grit and honesty.

Listen to what is being said when a friend flippantly drops a stinging remark about you. Observe how people react to you in a social gathering. Your co-workers' reactions towards you says a lot. Take the excruciating step and piece together how people really feel about you, including your family of origin. We can start to see things that we would never have allowed ourselves to see.

Not that all of these reactions about you are going to be true, not at all.

The vast majority of this precious information is not going to come up when things are going smoothly. Diamonds are made under pressure; rough seas make good sailors. No one ever said it was easy because, well, it's not.

But consider the alternative. Never seeing the truth about yourself. Not living up to your greatest potential. Never having the joyous life that was intended for you. How can you go and do the great things you want to do without knowing your strengths *and* your weaknesses?

19
Love like your life depends on it.

Coming from love is the most powerful act that can be done in the universe. A lot of people think that love is something optional to have in their lives. Nothing could be further from the truth. Don't wait to feel it to give it.

Acting in love should be as easy as breathing in and breathing out. It all comes back to this: everything you do, do out of love. Which is easier to do when you are receiving positive energy. The rubber hits the road when you are receiving anger or disappointment or mistrust. Those are the times when there is nothing else as important in your life than to act out of love.

Unlike being in love, conscious living in love does not require another participant, just you. Make a vow in the morning of each day that everything you say, think and do will reflect and contain only love regardless of what is said or done to you. If you find that you didn't live up to that, don't judge yourself and just gently bring yourself back to it.

Let your defenses down and don't worry if you are emotionally hurt by somebody else. Let go of your desires in this world and just focus on coming from a central place of love. In that way, what is truly yours will come to you. Whatever your job is, do it with honor. Be a good friend, work to end the systemic oppression of minorities, make this world a better place to live in. You will find so much more clarity than if you are just focusing on getting what you want.

When this pandemic is over, a question we will need to ask ourselves is if we want our world to return to the way it was before. Or do we want to use what we have gone through as a transformative moment in time and rebuild the world to better reflect our values? What does it say about America that many places in the world have already significantly brought down the number of infections?

By making this shift in your daily pursuits, you'll be taking on your true purpose on this planet. This is your true calling, your vocation. The life you save might be your own.

20
Find grace.

Finding grace in everything is the mirror image to feeling good.

There are things that happen on this planet that are terrible and unexplainable. Senseless violence that ends or completely alters people's lives. Random forces of nature that kill and injure thousands. Disease that infiltrates and stunts lives that once were thriving.

There are also certain kinds of hurts that happen to people that they are not going to be able to get beyond. It's not because it's impossible to, they're just not going to be able to.

It doesn't even have to be something big—something that seems small like an ill-fated interaction with another person can have a hurt that seems to go on and on.

We can scour books and search for the reason among the great teachers of the world. But ultimately it is up to each of us to create meaning in both the large tragedies and small setbacks that define our collective existence. To find grace in all that befalls us.

The meaning of these types of events is not going to just suddenly appear. Perhaps one meaning is that it allows us to be the grace in someone's tragedy. To be with people who are suffering so they know they are not alone. It's sometimes hard to find words for someone who has experienced a loss. But we can be there, even if it's mostly in silence, and hold a hand. To run an errand or make a meal. To say, "I don't know the reason why this happened, but you are my brother and sister, and you do not have to suffer alone".

Help to make the situation better. Donate to a charity. Speak up on social media. Volunteer your time. Keep in touch with people by calling and texting. Create meaning in these events by being a part of easing suffering and loneliness, by rebuilding and making a better world.

Find the grace. Be the grace.

21
There are a lot of things you won't finish.

Besides things like term papers, current year taxes, and some work projects, I'm not sure that we ever really finish anything (I've even had to go back and revise a filed tax return). We finally get what we wanted, a new car or gadget, and not long after, something catches our eye that's just a smidge more enticing and exciting. What has been dubbed "divine discontent" seems to be a part of the human condition—always wanting to experience that which hasn't been experienced yet. This can even apply to our romantic relationships.

It's satisfying when a task is actually able to be completed like painting a room. But there are so many more scenarios where it's not going to be like that. Published books are revised for a new edition, plays are tinkered with for the next revival. More often than not, the kinds of things we're responsible for are going to be like a living document that will need continuous updating.

We are creative beings and creation is not static, it is dynamic. It's easy to get frustrated that it seems like we're never really satisfied. There is always the latest device coming out, a new idea that expands upon our project at work, just one more home improvement that needs completing. It's more realistic to realize the universe is in constant motion and things are never going to stay the same. Yesterday's news is just that, today there is something new on the horizon. We have to engage in that balancing act of being happy with what we've achieved and have, and wanting to achieve more and have the latest and greatest.

There's always tomorrow to get a chance to make it better. Until that one day when there's not. So until then, embrace the certainty that life is about uncertainty and ride that wave. You'll never stop seeing new and glorious ways of being. Do all you can. Let go of what you can't. And laugh a lot.

22

Pay just enough attention to your dreams.

A common thread during this pandemic is the occurrence of vivid dreams. It's helpful to realize that the vast majority of dreams is your conscious and subconscious mind throwing up. It's mostly a lot of blah blah blah with a few substantive parts that warrant a looksee.

If you have the same dream or type of dream over and over, it doesn't take a dream interpreter to tell you to consider what that's all about. What pattern in your life is that a metaphor for? Often being able to consciously understand where that's coming from will cause those types of dreams to stop. Working on a personal issue and taking active steps to explore and release a hang-up are very helpful things to do.

For the most part our dreams are a scrambled way for our minds to release and vent. Don't get overwhelmed by it.

However, dream time can be a way that valuable information is being communicated to us. Our higher self sometimes gives us helpful tips about ourselves. Consider also that we all have a soul group, loving spirit guides who are and have been intertwined with us and want to provide assistance. One way of doing this is showing us things as we're dreaming when there is less distraction and resistance to it.

Sometimes we get an intuition about the future. Sometimes we get a warning. Sometimes we get a realization of who someone really is. Keep a notebook and pen next to your bed so if something really stands out you can write it down before it fades away. None of this is presented to rattle you, but rather to help you to take note and act accordingly if warranted.

23
Respect Mother Earth.

Our planet provides a wealth of precious resources that sustain a multitude of species. Humankind seems hell bent on taking much of those materials at a rate that is simply not sustainable. Facts are facts and people can bury their heads in the sand if they want but the truth is we are on a path of self-destruction and if we do not put in safeguards now to reverse global warming, life for all species is going to change in a very traumatic way. This planet will, in fact, become uninhabitable. We are now getting dire warnings about this by the number of and intensity of catastrophic storms and the increase of the average global temperature.

What is best is to regard the Earth as a living entity with an intelligence of her own. She is giving everything she can to sustain life and what is needed right now is a shift in consciousness that looks out for her best interests, which are also our own. Reversing global warming and stopping from being a throw-away society are not options, they are musts.

Respect our Mother. Allow her to go through the various phases and cycles she must go through. She is reacting to what is being done to her by creating equilibrium which is going to manifest in a variety of ways.

Do your part by living your life in a way that provides for the continuance of life on this planet for many generations. Honor her by keeping your consumption to what is absolutely necessary and replacing resources whenever possible. Recycle and reduce your carbon footprint. Bless her on her journey as we are on ours.

24
Accept the seeming paradoxes in life.

Have you ever noticed that self-help and spiritual concepts contain paradoxes? It's part of the reason they can be difficult to understand.

Here are some examples. Visualize what it is you want—but don't be attached to an outcome. Work hard—but don't have expectations for what you're going to receive. Do all these mental health exercises—but don't push it. Have the most noble of intentions—but the road to hell is paved with good intentions. You first have to accept yourself as you are in order to make the changes in yourself you want.

It's enough to make anyone throw their arms up in frustration. But if we truly want the best life possible, if we want to be the best version of ourselves that we can be, then we should quiet our minds and just be in acceptance.

Two concepts that appear to contradict each other can harmoniously co-exist. It is not one thing vs. another thing, or me against you. It is the fact that we are all one working in unanimity for the greater good. Give up the idea of competing tendencies and become immersed with being in the flow of all things working out in the best way possible for all. We always stand up for what is right as we accept that there is darkness among us.

Whatever ideal we a marching towards as the human race, whatever the pinnacle it is we want to achieve, we are not going to get there unless we are all building each other up and ensuring everyone has an equal status and a place at the table.

25
Make the conscious choice to be happy.

Life can feel like a fool's errand in which we're all just victims of happenstance. Honestly, what is it we can actually control? Not even our own thoughts most of the time. Being alive can feel like we're constantly in reactive mode stuck in the newest round of damage control. And now along comes a pandemic to finish off what was left of our sanity.

Our parents are getting older and our children are getting older and we're getting older. Years go by and then the decades. For the majority of us in this haphazard life, if we're going to be happy, we're going to have to choose to be happy. It is not a state that descends upon us when we have successfully maneuvered through all the obstacles before us. It is an inner directive, a conscious choice.

It is perhaps the only say that we really have in this world. We decree that despite all the slings and arrows, we choose to be happy.

With every task we are involved with, let us declare that we are happy. Let us take meditation breaks each day to remind ourselves that we have chosen happiness. Let us be both cheerleader and comforter to ourselves. We choose to have a little smile on our face everywhere we go. When we're hurting, we remember all that we have overcome and tell ourselves we're going to get through this one too.

Choosing happiness is our personal work of art in an indifferent world. Our way of defining ourselves that come what may, this is who we really are.

When people think of you, when they remember you, let that thought be that whatever life handed you, you remained kind and steadfast and trustworthy. That many trials may have befallen you, but you chose to keep the faith and be happy.

You are far more than you know. What you have gotten through is nothing short of extraordinary. The power that resides inside of you is phenomenal. Love yourself, never stop being the highest version of yourself in every moment, and shine your light on everything that you come in contact with.

I wish you peace and joy on your journey home.